Spelling
Handbook

k12

Book Staff and Contributors

Marianne Murphy   *Content Specialist*
David Shireman   *Instructional Designer*
Mary Beck Desmond   *Senior Text Editor*
Ron Stanley   *Text Editor*
Suzanne Montazer   *Creative Director, Print and ePublishing*
Sasha Blanton   *Senior Print Visual Designer*
Julie Jankowski, Eric Trott   *Print Visual Designers*
Stephanie Williams   *Cover Designer*
Tim Mansfield   *Writer*
Amy Eward   *Senior Manager, Writers*
Susan Raley   *Manager, Editors*
Colleen Line   *Senior Project Manager*

Maria Szalay   *Senior Vice President for Product Development*
John Holdren   *Senior Vice President for Content and Curriculum*
David Pelizzari   *Vice President, Content and Curriculum*
Kim Barcas   *Vice President, Creative*
Laura Seuschek   *Vice President, Instructional Design and Evaluation & Research*
Aaron Hall   *Vice President, Program Management*

Lisa Dimaio Iekel   *Production Manager*
John Agnone   *Director of Publications*

About K12 Inc.

K12 Inc., a technology-based education company, is the nation's leading provider of proprietary curriculum and online education programs to students in grades K–12. K12 provides its curriculum and academic services to online schools, traditional classrooms, blended school programs, and directly to families. K12 Inc. also operates the K12 International Academy, an accredited, diploma-granting online private school serving students worldwide. K12's mission is to provide any child the curriculum and tools to maximize success in life, regardless of geographic, financial, or demographic circumstances. K12 Inc. is accredited by CITA. More information can be found at www.K12.com.

978-1-60153-163-6
Printed by LSC Communications, Willard, OH, USA, May 2018

Contents

K¹² Language Arts Spelling Course Overview

Overview

My spelling is Wobbly. It's good spelling but it Wobbles, and the letters get in the wrong places. — A. A. MILNE

The goal of K¹² Language Arts Spelling is to ensure students don't wobble with their spelling the way Winnie-the-Pooh does. As an engaging, portable program that can be tailored to the individual needs of students, K¹² Spelling will help students master the conventions of spelling needed to be proficient readers and writers.

While many may wonder about the need for formal spelling instruction in the digital age, K¹² firmly believes in the power and necessity of mastering the traditional subject of spelling. K¹² Spelling focuses on learning to recognize patterns rather than memorizing rules—no spelling rule is 100 percent reliable. Research shows that good readers and spellers do not decode (read) and encode (spell) rules, but rather letter patterns that help them identify words and differentiate one word from another.

A great deal of research shows that continually revisiting and building on mastered concepts helps students master new concepts. With each subsequent grade level, spelling conventions build on previously mastered content while giving students many options for multimodal learning. Throughout grades 1–5, students build a strong foundation that leads to a strong storehouse of knowledge about spelling and the English language.

K¹² Spelling is designed to accommodate students who will master the content at different paces and who will require varying amounts of study. K¹² believes that students can learn to spell words quickly by studying spelling patterns that are common to many words. A certain number of common words fall outside these conventions, and students need to learn to spell those words quickly in preparation for the demands of grade-level writing requirements.

To balance the goals of learning to spell both within and outside spelling conventions, the spelling words in K¹² Spelling are divided into four categories: Heart Words, Target Words, Challenge Words, and Alternate Words.

Heart Words represent some of the most commonly spelled words outside the spelling conventions taught at each grade level. Other programs may refer to these as sight words, trick words, or snap words. Heart Words do not follow the spelling patterns being covered in the unit, but it is important for students to learn to spell these very common words that have to be learned "by heart." A unit will typically include two to four Heart Words. You will help students track which Heart Words they have mastered, and students will continue to study each Heart Word until they have mastered it. All students are expected to demonstrate mastery of Heart Words.

Target Words follow the spelling pattern being studied in a unit. For example, all Target Words for a given unit may be words that end with a double letter. Along with the Heart Words, these words represent the core content to be learned by students in a unit. A unit will present ten Target Words. All students are expected to demonstrate mastery of Target Words.

Challenge Words also follow the spelling convention being studied in any given unit, but are somewhat more difficult to spell. Challenge Words will be presented to students only if they first show mastery of the unit's Heart Words and Target Words. Each unit includes two to four Challenge Words. Not all students are expected to demonstrate mastery of Challenge Words.

Alternate Words are like Target Words and represent another set of words that follow the spelling convention being studied in the unit. Alternate Words are a source of extra words for students who show ready mastery of the Heart Words and Target Words. Ten Alternate Words are identified in most units. Not all students are expected to demonstrate mastery of Alternate Words.

Unit Plans

K[12] Spelling presents a cohesive, pattern-based program designed to enable you to guide students through the instruction of these four different types of words.

K[12] Spelling Green consists of 18 units. Each five-day unit focuses on a particular spelling convention and follows a set, repeated pattern.

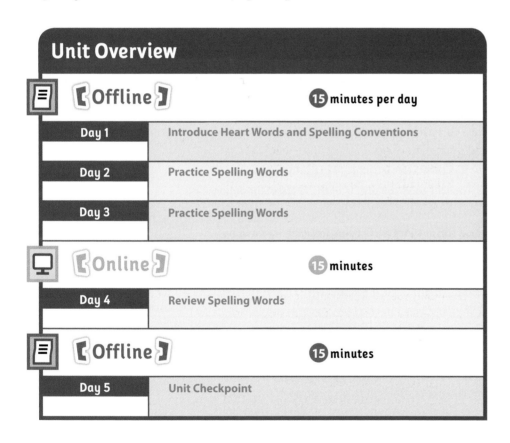

Unit Overview		
[Offline]		🕒 **15 minutes per day**
Day 1	Introduce Heart Words and Spelling Conventions	
Day 2	Practice Spelling Words	
Day 3	Practice Spelling Words	
[Online]		🕒 **15 minutes**
Day 4	Review Spelling Words	
[Offline]		🕒 **15 minutes**
Day 5	Unit Checkpoint	

Day 1

On Day 1, students' spelling list, or Words to Learn, is determined. Students will take a pretest, establishing their initial level of mastery of the spelling words presented in that unit. You will then guide students through the discovery of the spelling convention being studied in that unit, and students will briefly practice the spelling words that they did not master in the pretest.

Day 2

You will use the Activity Bank to practice spelling words with students. The Activity Bank is a collection of interactive, offline activities designed to allow students to practice spelling words in a variety of ways. You can choose any of the activities in the Activity Bank to do on Days 2 and 3 of the unit, so try out as many of the activities as possible to discover which ones motivate and produce the best learning for your students.

Day 3

You will use the Activity Bank to practice spelling words with students. You are encouraged, but not required, to choose activities different from those you used on Day 2.

Day 4

Students will play an online game in which they review the spelling words in the unit. At the beginning of the game, you will choose whether the game should present only the Heart Words and Target Words to students, or whether Challenge Words or Alternate Words should also be included. This online review serves as preparation for the assessment (Unit Checkpoint) on Day 5.

Day 5

Students will complete an offline Unit Checkpoint covering the Heart Words and Target Words from the unit. Only the Heart Words and Target Words are assessed because they represent the core content of the course. You will enter the results of the assessment online to track student progress.

Since each unit follows the same pattern, full activity directions for each day will be repeated only in the first two Unit Plans. In subsequent units, an abbreviated version of the instructions is presented. However, the spelling words, materials lists, advance preparation, and any guidance particular to a unit will be presented in each specific Unit Plan.

Semester Review

The final unit in K[12] Spelling is a semester review unit. The review unit consists of the same introduction, practice, and assessment procedures as other units. But instead of introducing a new spelling convention, it reviews the spelling conventions studied in the previous units. All of the words are made up of a selection of words from previous units representing each of the spelling conventions covered.

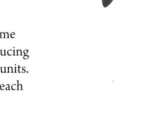

Spelling
Handbook

Heart Words and CVC Words

Target spelling convention – **one beginning consonant + one middle vowel + one ending consonant**

When a word has only one vowel followed by one or more consonants, the vowel sound is usually short. We call these words consonant-vowel-consonant words, or CVC words. This unit's spelling words are all CVC words.

Objectives
- Spell Heart Words.
- Spell CVC words.

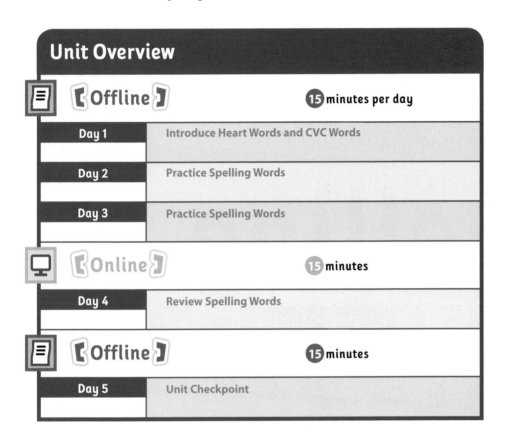

Unit Overview

▤ 〔Offline〕 ⑮ minutes per day

Day 1	Introduce Heart Words and CVC Words
Day 2	Practice Spelling Words
Day 3	Practice Spelling Words

🖥 〔Online〕 ⑮ minutes

| Day 4 | Review Spelling Words |

▤ 〔Offline〕 ⑮ minutes

| Day 5 | Unit Checkpoint |

♡ Heart Words

I   a

✰ Challenge Words

tomcat   cobweb   suntan

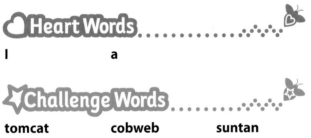

◎ Target Words

man	top	red
can	fix	yes
six	fun	hot
sun		

Alternate Words

bad	cup	did
met	hat	box
win	ten	cut
nod		

Offline 🕙 minutes per day

Complete the Spelling activities with students.

Introduce Heart Words and CVC Words

* index cards (25)
* whiteboard (optional)

Advance Preparation

Write each Heart, Target, Challenge, and Alternate Word on a separate index card. Use small symbols or letters to indicate which type of word is written on each card. For example, you can use a T for Target Words, a heart symbol for Heart Words, a C for Challenge Words, and an A for Alternate Words.

| T shop | ♡ a | C suntan | A dock |

Pretest

1. Using the index cards you prepared, **say** each Heart and Target Word and have students write it on a whiteboard or sheet of paper. As you give the pretest, place the cards for words students spelled correctly in a Mastered pile. Place the cards for words students misspelled in a Words to Learn pile.

2. **Gather** the cards for all the words students have misspelled, which will be students' Words to Learn for this unit. It is best if students have between 10 and 20 Words to Learn, depending on students' rate of mastery.

   ► If students misspelled only a few words, consider adding a few Alternate or Challenge Words.
   ► If students didn't misspell any Heart or Target Words, give them a pretest using the Alternate and Challenge Words. Add the words they misspell to their Words to Learn.

Note: If students didn't misspell any Heart, Target, Challenge, or Alternate Words, mark Lessons 2 and 3 complete and move to the online activity for Day 4 to practice for the Unit Checkpoint on Day 5.

Heart Words

Heart Words do not follow spelling conventions, so we learn them "by heart."

➲ *Skip this activity if students didn't misspell any Heart Words on this unit's pretest.*

1. **Gather** the Words to Learn cards for any Heart Words.

2. **Practice** the Heart Words.

   ► Have students choose a card and read the word aloud.

     Successful?
     • Cover the card and have students write the word on a whiteboard or sheet of paper.
     • Go to the next word.

     Not successful?
     • Say the word and have students spell it aloud.
     • Have students picture the letters of the word in their mind.
     • Have students write the word on a whiteboard or sheet of paper.
     • Have students spell the word aloud again.

   ► Continue this way through all the Heart Words for this unit.

3. **Track mastery** of Heart Words.

   ► When students read and spell a Heart Word correctly, mark the index card with the date.
   ► When any index card has three dates marked on it, that card should be moved from the group of Heart Words students are still working on to the group of Heart Words students have mastered.

Target Words

Target Words have the single spelling convention we're focusing on in this lesson.

➲ *Skip this activity if students didn't misspell any Target Words on this unit's pretest.*

1. **Gather** the Words to Learn cards for any Target Words.

2. **Discover** the new spelling convention.

   ► Explain the new spelling convention described at the beginning of this unit.
   ► Have students search for the new spelling convention in the words on the index cards.
   ► Say and discuss the new spelling convention in each Target Word.
   ► Have students picture the letters of the word in their mind.

3. **Practice** the Target Words.

   ► Have students sound out the Target Words.
   ► Have students point out the spelling convention in the words.
   ► Say a word and have students spell it aloud.

- Go to the next word.

- Review the correct spelling with students.
- Have students write the word on a whiteboard or sheet of paper.
- Have students spell the word aloud again.

▶ Continue this way through all the Target Words for this unit.

Challenge Words

Challenge Words follow the unit's spelling convention, but are more difficult than the Target Words.

⮌ *Skip this activity if students are struggling with the Heart Words and Target Words.*

1. **Gather** the Words to Learn cards for any Challenge Words.

2. **Discover** the new spelling convention in the Challenge Words.

   ▶ Explain the new spelling convention described at the beginning of this unit.
   ▶ Have students search for the new spelling convention in the words on the index cards.
   ▶ Say each word and have students spell it aloud.
   ▶ Have students picture the letters of each word in their mind.

3. **Practice** the Challenge Words.

   ▶ Have students write the word on a whiteboard or sheet of paper.
   ▶ Have students spell the word aloud again.

Alternate Words

Alternate Words follow the unit's spelling convention.

⮌ *Skip this activity if students don't have any Words to Learn cards for Alternate Words.*

1. **Gather** the Words to Learn cards for any Alternate Words.

2. **Discover** the new spelling convention in the Alternate Words.

   ▶ Explain the new spelling convention described at the beginning of this unit.
   ▶ Have students search for the new spelling convention in the words on the index cards.
   ▶ Say each word and have students spell it aloud.
   ▶ Have students picture the letters of each word in their mind.

3. **Practice** the Alternate Words.

   ▶ Have students write the word on a whiteboard or sheet of paper.
   ▶ Have students spell the word aloud again.

Practice Spelling Words

Students need to practice only the words on their Words to Learn cards from Day 1.

1. **Choose** a spelling activity from the Activity Bank on pages **SP 78–82**.

2. **Use** *all* the Words to Learn during the activity.

3. **Choose** a second activity if you have time.

Practice Spelling Words

Follow the same procedure as on Day 2, but choose different activities from the Activity Bank.

 **15 minutes**

Review Spelling Words

Help students **find the online review activity**, choose Challenge Words or Alternate Words if students have studied those words this unit, and provide support as needed.

[Offline] ⏱ **15 minutes**

Day 5

Unit Checkpoint

Students will complete an offline Unit Checkpoint covering the Heart Words and Target Words from the unit. (Challenge Words and Alternate Words are not included on the Checkpoint.)

1. **Dictate** the Heart Words and Target Words.

   ‣ Have students write the words on a sheet of paper.

2. **Check** students' answers.

   ‣ Circle the words students spell incorrectly.
   ‣ Enter students' results online.

3. **Review** the words students misspelled.

   ‣ Gather these Words to Learn cards and put them aside for further practice as time allows.

 Reward: If students scored 80 percent or above on the Unit Checkpoint, add a sticker to the Unit 1 box on students' My Accomplishments chart. If students scored under 80 percent, continue to practice the words that they missed and add a sticker to this unit once they have mastered the words.

Heart Words and Double Trouble Words

Target spelling convention – **one vowel + double letters**

The letters *f, l, s,* and *z* are usually doubled at the end of short words that have only one vowel. But we say the sound only once when we read these words. This unit's spelling words all end with double letters.

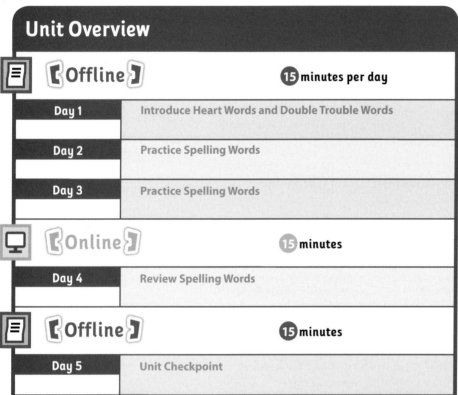

Unit Overview

[Offline] — **15** minutes per day

Day 1	Introduce Heart Words and Double Trouble Words
Day 2	Practice Spelling Words
Day 3	Practice Spelling Words

[Online] — **15** minutes

| Day 4 | Review Spelling Words |

[Offline] — **15** minutes

| Day 5 | Unit Checkpoint |

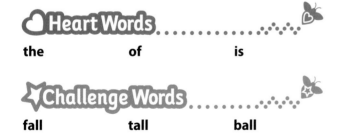

Heart Words

the	of	is

Challenge Words

fall	tall	ball

Target Words

will	tell	puff
fizz	miss	boss
off	kiss	well
pass		

Alternate Words

pull	wall	loss
less	cuff	fuzz
fill	buzz	toss
mass		

 **15** minute per day

Complete the Spelling activities with students.

Day 1

Introduce Heart Words and Double Trouble Words

- index cards (26)
- whiteboard (optional)

Advance Preparation

Write each Heart, Target, Challenge, and Alternate Word on a separate index card. Use small symbols or letters to indicate which type of word is written on each card. For example, you can use a T for Target Words, a heart symbol for Heart Words, a C for Challenge Words, and an A for Alternate Words.

 shop   a   suntan   dock

Pretest

1. Using the index cards you prepared, **say** each Heart and Target Word and have students write it on a whiteboard or sheet of paper. As you give the pretest, place the cards for words students spelled correctly in a Mastered pile. Place the cards for words students misspelled in a Words to Learn pile.

2. **Gather** the cards for all the words students have misspelled, which will be students' Words to Learn for this unit. It is best if students have between 10 and 20 Words to Learn, depending on students' rate of mastery.

   ▸ If students misspelled only a few words, consider adding a few Alternate or Challenge Words.
   ▸ If students didn't misspell any Heart or Target Words, give them a pretest using the Alternate and Challenge Words. Add the words they misspell to their Words to Learn.

Note: If students didn't misspell any Heart, Target, Challenge, or Alternate Words, mark Lessons 2 and 3 complete and move to the online activity for Day 4 to practice for the Unit Checkpoint on Day 5.

Heart Words

Heart Words do not follow spelling conventions, so we learn them "by heart."

⮕ *Skip this activity if students didn't misspell any Heart Words on this unit's pretest.*

1. **Gather** the Words to Learn cards for any new Heart Words.

2. **Practice** the *new* Heart Words.

   ▸ Have students choose a card and read the word aloud.

   Successful?
   • Cover the card and have students write the word on a whiteboard or sheet of paper.
   • Go to the next word.

   Not successful?
   • Say the word and have students spell it aloud.
   • Have students picture the letters of the word in their mind.
   • Have students write the word again on a whiteboard or sheet of paper.
   • Have students spell the word aloud again.

   ▸ Continue this way through all the new Heart Words for this unit.

3. **Practice** *all* Heart Words.

   ▸ Add the new Heart Words to the Words to Learn cards of all the Heart Words students have not yet mastered.
   ▸ Have students choose a card and read the word aloud.

   Successful?
   • Cover the card and have students write it on a whiteboard or sheet of paper.
   • Go to the next word.

   Not successful?
   • Say the word and have students spell it aloud.
   • Have students picture the letters of the word in their mind.
   • Have students write the word again on a whiteboard or sheet of paper.
   • Have students spell the word aloud again.

   ▸ Continue this way through all Heart Words students have not yet mastered.

4. **Track mastery** of Heart Words.

   ▸ When students read and spell a Heart Word correctly, mark the index card with the date.
   ▸ When any index card has three dates marked on it, that card should be moved from the group of Heart Words students are still working on to the group of Heart Words students have mastered.

Target Words

Target Words have the single spelling convention we're focusing on in this lesson.

⮌ *Skip this activity if students didn't misspell any Target Words on this unit's pretest.*

1. **Gather** the Words to Learn cards for any Target Words.

2. **Discover** the new spelling convention.

   ▸ Explain the new spelling convention described at the beginning of this unit.
   ▸ Have students search for the new spelling convention in the words on the index cards.
   ▸ Say and discuss the new spelling convention in each Target Word.
   ▸ Have students picture the letters of the word in their mind.

3. **Practice** the Target Words.

> ▸ Have students sound out the Target Words.
> ▸ Have students point out the spelling convention in the words.
> ▸ Say a word and have students spell it aloud.
>
> **Successful?**
> • Go to the next word.
>
> **Not successful?**
> • Review the correct spelling with students.
> • Have students write the word on a whiteboard or sheet of paper.
> • Have students spell the word aloud again.
>
> ▸ Continue this way through all the Target Words for this unit.

Challenge Words

Challenge Words follow the unit's spelling convention, but are more difficult than the Target Words.

➲ *Skip this activity if students are struggling with the Heart Words and Target Words.*

1. **Gather** the Words to Learn cards for any Challenge Words.

2. **Discover** the new spelling convention in the Challenge Words.

> ▸ Explain the new spelling convention described at the beginning of this unit.
> ▸ Have students search for the new spelling convention in the words on the index cards.
> ▸ Say each word and have students spell it aloud.
> ▸ Have students picture the letters of each word in their mind.

3. **Practice** the Challenge Words.

> ▸ Have students write the word on a whiteboard or sheet of paper.
> ▸ Have students spell the word aloud again.

Alternate Words

Alternate Words follow the unit's spelling convention.

➲ *Skip this activity if students don't have any Words to Learn cards for Alternate Words.*

1. **Gather** the Words to Learn cards for any Alternate Words.

2. **Discover** the new spelling convention in the Alternate Words.

> ▸ Explain the new spelling convention described at the beginning of this unit.
> ▸ Have students search for the new spelling convention in the words on the index cards.
> ▸ Say each word and have students spell it aloud.
> ▸ Have students picture the letters of each word in their mind.

3. **Practice** the Alternate Words.

> ▸ Have students write the word on a whiteboard or sheet of paper.
> ▸ Ask students to spell the word aloud again.

Day 2

Practice Spelling Words

Students need to practice only the words on their Words to Learn cards from Day 1.

1. **Choose** a spelling activity from the Activity Bank on pages **SP 78–82**.

2. **Use** *all* the Words to Learn during the activity.

3. **Choose** a second activity if you have time.

Day 3

Practice Spelling Words

Follow the same procedure as on Day 2, but choose different activities from the Activity Bank.

 **15 minutes**

Day 4

Review Spelling Words

Help students **find the online review activity**, choose Challenge Words or Alternate Words if students have studied those words this unit, and provide support as needed.

[Offline] ⏱ minutes

Unit Checkpoint

Students will complete an offline Unit Checkpoint covering the Heart Words and Target Words from the unit. (Challenge Words and Alternate Words are not included on the Checkpoint.)

1. **Dictate** the Heart Words and Target Words.

   ▸ Have students write the words on a sheet of paper.

2. **Check** students' answers.

   ▸ Circle the words students spell incorrectly.
   ▸ Enter students' results online.

3. **Review** the words students misspelled.

   ▸ Gather these Words to Learn cards and put them aside for further practice as time allows.

Reward: If students scored 80 percent or above on the Unit Checkpoint, add a sticker to the Unit 2 box on students' My Accomplishments chart. If students scored under 80 percent, continue to practice the words that they missed and add a sticker to this unit once they have mastered the words.

Heart Words and Digraph *ck*

Target spelling convention — **the single sound created by the letter combination *ck***

When a one-syllable word with a short vowel ends in a /k/ sound, /k/ is spelled *ck*. This unit's words all end with the letters *ck*.

Unit Overview

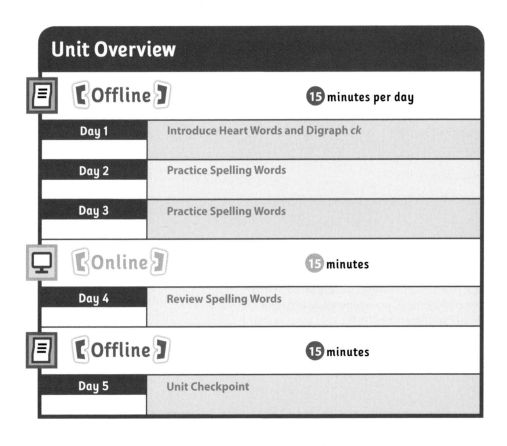

Offline		**15 minutes per day**
Day 1	Introduce Heart Words and Digraph *ck*	
Day 2	Practice Spelling Words	
Day 3	Practice Spelling Words	
Online		**15 minutes**
Day 4	Review Spelling Words	
Offline		**15 minutes**
Day 5	Unit Checkpoint	

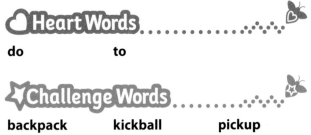

♡ Heart Words

do	to

☆ Challenge Words

backpack	kickball	pickup

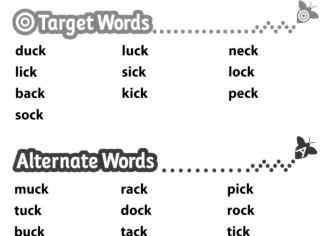

◎ Target Words

duck	luck	neck
lick	sick	lock
back	kick	peck
sock		

Alternate Words

muck	rack	pick
tuck	dock	rock
buck	tack	tick
sack		

 **15** minutes per day

Complete the Spelling activities with students. **For the full instructions for each activity, refer to pages SP 8–13.**

Day 1

Introduce Heart Words and Digraph *ck*

- index cards (25)
- whiteboard (optional)

Advance Preparation

Write each Heart, Target, Challenge, and Alternate Word on a separate index card. Indicate on each card whether a word is a Heart, Target, Challenge, or Alternate Word.

Pretest

1. **Administer** a pretest using the Heart and Target Words.

2. **Gather** students' Words to Learn cards.

Note: If students didn't misspell any Heart, Target, Challenge, or Alternate Words, mark Lessons 2 and 3 complete and move to the online activity for Day 4 to practice for the Unit Checkpoint on Day 5.

Heart Words

➲ *Skip this activity if students didn't misspell any Heart Words on this unit's pretest.*

1. **Gather** the Words to Learn cards for any Heart Words.

2. **Practice** the *new* Heart Words.

3. **Practice** *all* Heart Words.

4. **Track mastery** of Heart Words.

Target Words

➲ *Skip this activity if students didn't misspell any Target Words on this unit's pretest.*

1. **Gather** the Words to Learn cards for any Target Words.

2. **Discover** the new spelling convention.

3. **Practice** the Target Words.

Challenge Words

⮑ *Skip this activity if students are struggling with the Heart Words and Target Words.*

1. **Gather** the Words to Learn cards for any Challenge Words.
2. **Discover** the new spelling convention in the Challenge Words.
3. **Practice** the Challenge Words.

Alternate Words

⮑ *Skip this activity if students don't have any Words to Learn cards for Alternate Words.*

1. **Gather** the Words to Learn cards for any Alternate Words.
2. **Discover** the new spelling convention in the Alternate Words.
3. **Practice** the Alternate Words.

Day 2 . . . .

Practice Spelling Words

Practice using the Activity Bank.

Day 3 . . . .

Practice Spelling Words

Practice using the Activity Bank.

 **⑮ minutes**

Day 4 . . . .

Review Spelling Words

Review using the online activity.

 **15** minutes

Unit Checkpoint

1. **Dictate** the Heart Words and Target Words.

2. **Check** students' answers.

3. **Review** the words students misspelled.

 Reward: If students scored 80 percent or above on the Unit Checkpoint, add a sticker to the Unit 3 box on students' My Accomplishments chart. If students scored under 80 percent, continue to practice the words that they missed and add a sticker to this unit once they have mastered the words.

Heart Words and Regular Plurals

Target spelling convention — **creating plurals with *s* or *es***

To make most words plural, we add the ending –*s*. To make words that end in the letters *x* or *ss* plural, we add the ending –*es*. This unit's words all have the ending –*s* or –*es* added to a base word.

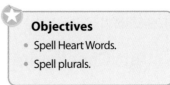

Objectives
- Spell Heart Words.
- Spell plurals.

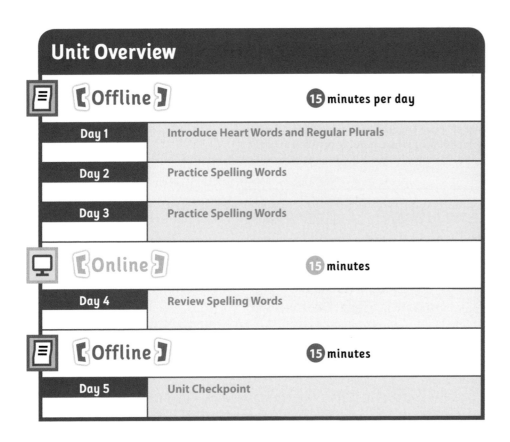

Unit Overview		
[Offline]		**15** minutes per day
Day 1	Introduce Heart Words and Regular Plurals	
Day 2	Practice Spelling Words	
Day 3	Practice Spelling Words	
[Online]		**15** minutes
Day 4	Review Spelling Words	
[Offline]		**15** minutes
Day 5	Unit Checkpoint	

⬭ Heart Words

as	has	his

☆ Challenge Words

dresses	packs	bluffs

◎ Target Words

runs	dogs	boxes
pills	pins	bells
rocks	kisses	
kids	misses	

Alternate Words

cats	hisses	bosses
messes	hens	hogs
hugs	rats	foxes
dolls		

 **15** minutes per day

Complete the Spelling activities with students. **For the full instructions for each activity, refer to pages SP 8–13.**

For the full instructions for each activity, refer to pages SP 8–13.

Day 1

Introduce Heart Words and Regular Plurals

Materials

- index cards (26)
- whiteboard (optional)

Advance Preparation

Write each Heart, Target, Challenge, and Alternate Word on a separate index card. Indicate on each card whether a word is a Heart, Target, Challenge, or Alternate Word.

Pretest

1. **Administer** a pretest using the Heart and Target Words.

2. **Gather** students' Words to Learn cards.

Note: If students didn't misspell any Heart, Target, Challenge, or Alternate Words, mark Lessons 2 and 3 complete and move to the online activity for Day 4 to practice for the Unit Checkpoint on Day 5.

Heart Words

↻ *Skip this activity if students didn't misspell any Heart Words on this unit's pretest.*

1. **Gather** the Words to Learn cards for any Heart Words.

2. **Practice** the *new* Heart Words.

3. **Practice** *all* Heart Words.

4. **Track mastery** of Heart Words.

Target Words

↻ *Skip this activity if students didn't misspell any Target Words on this unit's pretest.*

1. **Gather** the Words to Learn cards for any Target Words.

2. **Discover** the new spelling convention.

3. **Practice** the Target Words.

Challenge Words

↪ *Skip this activity if students are struggling with the Heart Words and Target Words.*

1. **Gather** the Words to Learn cards for any Challenge Words.
2. **Discover** the new spelling convention in the Challenge Words.
3. **Practice** the Challenge Words.

Alternate Words

↪ *Skip this activity if students don't have any Words to Learn cards for Alternate Words.*

1. **Gather** the Words to Learn cards for any Alternate Words.
2. **Discover** the new spelling convention in the Alternate Words.
3. **Practice** the Alternate Words.

Day 2 . . . .

Practice Spelling Words

Practice using the Activity Bank.

Day 3 . . . .

Practice Spelling Words

Practice using the Activity Bank.

 **15 minutes**

Day 4 . . . .

Review Spelling Words

Review using the online activity.

 **15** minutes

Day 5

Unit Checkpoint

1. **Dictate** the Heart Words and Target Words.

2. **Check** students' answers.

3. **Review** the words students misspelled.

Reward: If students scored 80 percent or above on the Unit Checkpoint, add a sticker to the Unit 4 box on students' My Accomplishments chart. If students scored under 80 percent, continue to practice the words that they missed and add a sticker to this unit once they have mastered the words.

Heart Words and Digraphs *th* & *wh*

Target spelling convention – **the single sound made by the letter combination *th*; the single sound made by the letter combination *wh***

When we use two letters to make one sound, we call the letters a digraph. The letters *th* are a digraph. They spell the soft /th/ sound in *think* and the hard /<u>th</u>/ sound in *this*. The letters *wh* are also a digraph. They spell the /w/ sounds in the words *when* and *where*. This unit's words all contain the digraph *th* or *wh*.

Objectives
- Spell Heart Words.
- Spell words containing the digraph *th*.
- Spell words containing the digraph *wh*.

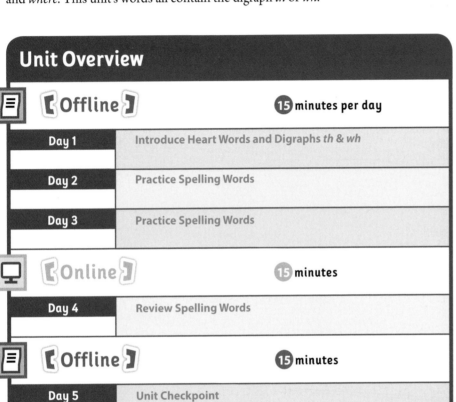

Unit Overview

[Offline] — 15 minutes per day

Day 1	Introduce Heart Words and Digraphs *th* & *wh*
Day 2	Practice Spelling Words
Day 3	Practice Spelling Words

[Online] — 15 minutes

Day 4	Review Spelling Words

[Offline] — 15 minutes

Day 5	Unit Checkpoint

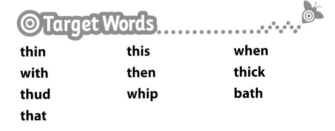

Heart Words

what	why	which

Challenge Words

they	there	both

Target Words

thin	this	when
with	then	thick
thud	whip	bath
that		

Alternate Words

math	thus	whim
thug	cloth	

[Offline] (15) minutes per day

Complete the Spelling activities with students. **For the full instructions for each activity, refer to pages SP 8–13.**

Day 1

Introduce Heart Words and Digraphs *th* & *wh*

Advance Preparation

Write each Heart, Target, Challenge, and Alternate Word on a separate index card. Indicate on each card whether a word is a Heart, Target, Challenge, or Alternate Word.

[Materials]

- index cards (21)
- whiteboard (optional)

Pretest

1. **Administer** a pretest using the Heart and Target Words.
2. **Gather** students' Words to Learn cards.

Note: If students didn't misspell any Heart, Target, Challenge, or Alternate Words, mark Lessons 2 and 3 complete and move to the online activity for Day 4 to practice for the Unit Checkpoint on Day 5.

Heart Words

⮑ *Skip this activity if students didn't misspell any Heart Words on this unit's pretest.*

1. **Gather** the Words to Learn cards for any Heart Words.
2. **Practice** the *new* Heart Words.
3. **Practice** *all* Heart Words.
4. **Track mastery** of Heart Words.

Target Words

⮑ *Skip this activity if students didn't misspell any Target Words on this unit's pretest.*

1. **Gather** the Words to Learn cards for any Target Words.
2. **Discover** the new spelling convention.
3. **Practice** the Target Words.

Challenge Words

↪ *Skip this activity if students are struggling with the Heart Words and Target Words.*

1. **Gather** the Words to Learn cards for any Challenge Words.
2. **Discover** the new spelling convention in the Challenge Words.
3. **Practice** the Challenge Words.

Alternate Words

↪ *Skip this activity if students don't have any Words to Learn cards for Alternate Words.*

1. **Gather** the Words to Learn cards for any Alternate Words.
2. **Discover** the new spelling convention in the Alternate Words.
3. **Practice** the Alternate Words.

Day 2

Practice Spelling Words

Practice using the Activity Bank.

Day 3

Practice Spelling Words

Practice using the Activity Bank.

 **15 minutes**

Day 4

Review Spelling Words

Review using the online activity.

 **15 minutes**

Unit Checkpoint

1. **Dictate** the Heart Words and Target Words.

2. **Check** students' answers.

3. **Review** the words students misspelled.

 Reward: If students scored 80 percent or above on the Unit Checkpoint, add a sticker to the Unit 5 box on students' My Accomplishments chart. If students scored under 80 percent, continue to practice the words that they missed and add a sticker to this unit once they have mastered the words.

Heart Words and Digraphs *sh & ch*

Target spelling convention – **the single sound made by the letter combination *sh*; the single sound made by the letter combination *ch***

The letters *sh* are a digraph. They spell the /sh/ sound in *shout* and *should*. The letters *ch* are also a digraph. They spell the /ch/ sound in the words *champ* and *chew*. This unit's words all contain the digraph *sh* or *ch*.

Objectives
- Spell Heart Words.
- Spell words containing the digraph *sh*.
- Spell words containing the digraph *ch*.

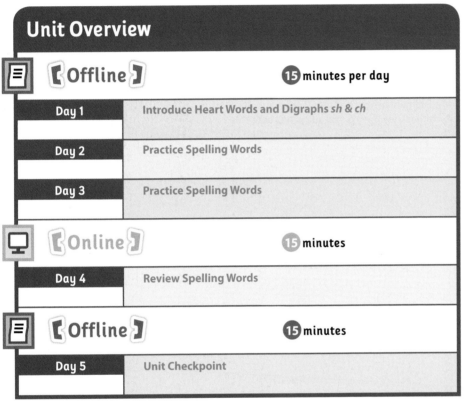

Unit Overview

📋 **〖Offline〗**		🕐 **minutes per day**
Day 1	Introduce Heart Words and Digraphs *sh & ch*	
Day 2	Practice Spelling Words	
Day 3	Practice Spelling Words	

🖥 **〖Online〗**		🕐 **minutes**
Day 4	Review Spelling Words	

📋 **〖Offline〗**		🕐 **minutes**
Day 5	Unit Checkpoint	

💭 Heart Words

be	me	she

⭐ Challenge Words

shellfish	whiplash	dishpan

◎ Target Words

shop	such	chess
ship	rush	much
wish	shut	chin
check		

Alternate Words

gush	lash	cash
chat	chop	shock
mash	shot	shack
chick		

Complete the Spelling activities with students. **For the full instructions for each activity, refer to pages SP 8–13.**

Day 1

Introduce Heart Words and Digraphs *sh & ch*

[Materials]

- index cards (26)
- whiteboard (optional)

Advance Preparation

Write each Heart, Target, Challenge, and Alternate Word on a separate index card. Indicate on each card whether a word is a Heart, Target, Challenge, or Alternate Word.

Pretest

1. **Administer** a pretest using the Heart and Target Words.

2. **Gather** students' Words to Learn cards.

Note: If students didn't misspell any Heart, Target, Challenge, or Alternate Words, mark Lessons 2 and 3 complete and move to the online activity for Day 4 to practice for the Unit Checkpoint on Day 5.

Heart Words

⊃ *Skip this activity if students didn't misspell any Heart Words on this unit's pretest.*

1. **Gather** the Words to Learn cards for any Heart Words.

2. **Practice** the *new* Heart Words.

3. **Practice** *all* Heart Words.

4. **Track mastery** of Heart Words.

Target Words

⊃ *Skip this activity if students didn't misspell any Target Words on this unit's pretest.*

1. **Gather** the Words to Learn cards for any Target Words.

2. **Discover** the new spelling convention.

3. **Practice** the Target Words.

Challenge Words

⮑ *Skip this activity if students are struggling with the Heart Words and Target Words.*

1. **Gather** the Words to Learn cards for any Challenge Words.

2. **Discover** the new spelling convention in the Challenge Words.

3. **Practice** the Challenge Words.

Alternate Words

⮑ *Skip this activity if students don't have any Words to Learn cards for Alternate Words.*

1. **Gather** the Words to Learn cards for any Alternate Words.

2. **Discover** the new spelling convention in the Alternate Words.

3. **Practice** the Alternate Words.

Day 2 ....

Practice Spelling Words

Practice using the Activity Bank.

Day 3 ....

Practice Spelling Words

Practice using the Activity Bank.

 **15** minutes

Day 4 ....

Review Spelling Words

Review using the online activity.

 **15 minutes**

Day 5

Unit Checkpoint

1. **Dictate** the Heart Words and Target Words.

2. **Check** students' answers.

3. **Review** the words students misspelled.

 Reward: If students scored 80 percent or above on the Unit Checkpoint, add a sticker to the Unit 6 box on students' My Accomplishments chart. If students scored under 80 percent, continue to practice the words that they missed and add a sticker to this unit once they have mastered the words.

Heart Words and Ending Blends

Target spelling convention — words ending in two consonants whose sounds blend together

Some words contain two consonants whose sounds blend together. We say that these words contain a consonant blend because the sounds of both consonants can be heard. Before we spell a word with a consonant blend, we have to listen carefully to the two sounds in the blend. This unit's words all end in a consonant blend.

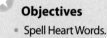

Objectives
- Spell Heart Words.
- Spell words ending in a consonant blend.

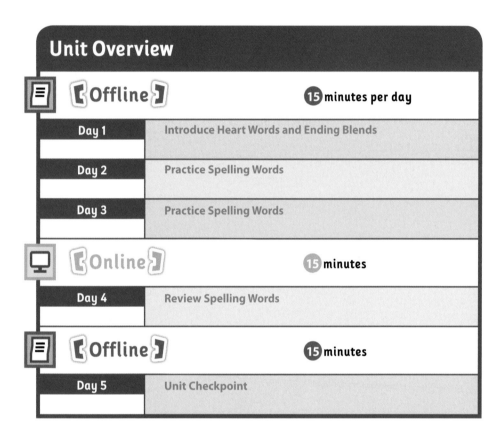

Unit Overview

Offline — 15 minutes per day

Day 1	Introduce Heart Words and Ending Blends
Day 2	Practice Spelling Words
Day 3	Practice Spelling Words

Online — 15 minutes

| Day 4 | Review Spelling Words |

Offline — 15 minutes

| Day 5 | Unit Checkpoint |

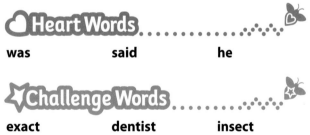

Heart Words

| was | said | he |

Challenge Words

| exact | dentist | insect |

Target Words

gift	held	just
self	camp	hand
next	milk	end
belt		

Alternate Words

fact	soft	must
lamp	shelf	nest
act	risk	best
lift		

 **15 minutes per day**

Complete the Spelling activities with students. **For the full instructions for each activity, refer to pages SP 8–13.**

Day 1

Introduce Heart Words and Ending Blends

Materials

• index cards (26)
• whiteboard (optional)

Advance Preparation

Write each Heart, Target, Challenge, and Alternate Word on a separate index card. Indicate on each card whether a word is a Heart, Target, Challenge, or Alternate Word.

Pretest

1. **Administer** a pretest using the Heart and Target Words.

2. **Gather** students' Words to Learn cards.

Note: If students didn't misspell any Heart, Target, Challenge, or Alternate Words, mark Lessons 2 and 3 complete and move to the online activity for Day 4 to practice for the Unit Checkpoint on Day 5.

Heart Words

➲ *Skip this activity if students didn't misspell any Heart Words on this unit's pretest.*

1. **Gather** the Words to Learn cards for any Heart Words.

2. **Practice** the *new* Heart Words.

3. **Practice** *all* Heart Words.

4. **Track mastery** of Heart Words.

Target Words

➲ *Skip this activity if students didn't misspell any Target Words on this unit's pretest.*

1. **Gather** the Words to Learn cards for any Target Words.

2. **Discover** the new spelling convention.

3. **Practice** the Target Words.

Challenge Words

⟳ *Skip this activity if students are struggling with the Heart Words and Target Words.*

1. **Gather** the Words to Learn cards for any Challenge Words.
2. **Discover** the new spelling convention in the Challenge Words.
3. **Practice** the Challenge Words.

Alternate Words

⟳ *Skip this activity if students don't have any Words to Learn cards for Alternate Words.*

1. **Gather** the Words to Learn cards for any Alternate Words.
2. **Discover** the new spelling convention in the Alternate Words.
3. **Practice** the Alternate Words.

Day 2 ....

Practice Spelling Words

Practice using the Activity Bank.

Day 3 ....

Practice Spelling Words

Practice using the Activity Bank.

 **15 minutes**

Day 4 ....

Review Spelling Words

Review using the online activity.

Day 5

Unit Checkpoint

1. **Dictate** the Heart Words and Target Words.

2. **Check** students' answers.

3. **Review** the words students misspelled.

Reward: If students scored 80 percent or above on the Unit Checkpoint, add a sticker to the Unit 7 box on students' My Accomplishments chart. If students scored under 80 percent, continue to practice the words that they missed and add a sticker to this unit once they have mastered the words.

Heart Words and Beginning Blends

Target spelling convention – **words beginning with two consonants whose sounds blend together**

Some words contain two consonants whose sounds blend together. We say that these words contain a consonant blend because the sounds of both consonants can be heard. Before we spell a word with a consonant blend, we have to listen carefully to the two sounds in the blend. This unit's words all begin with a consonant blend.

Objectives
- Spell Heart Words.
- Spell words beginning with a consonant blend.

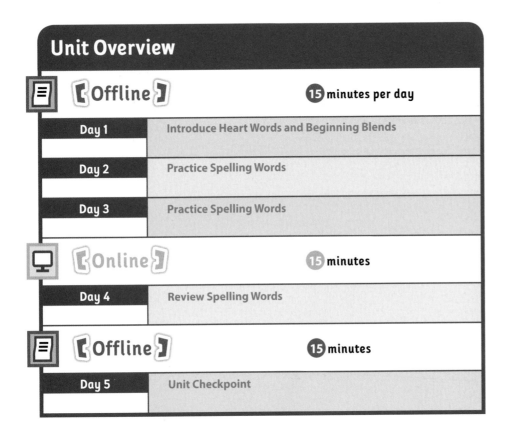

Unit Overview

	⎡Offline⎤	**15 minutes per day**
Day 1	Introduce Heart Words and Beginning Blends	
Day 2	Practice Spelling Words	
Day 3	Practice Spelling Words	

	⎡Online⎤	**15 minutes**
Day 4	Review Spelling Words	

	⎡Offline⎤	**15 minutes**
Day 5	Unit Checkpoint	

☁Heart Words

push   from

☆Challenge Words

draft   twist

◎Target Words

black	swim	truck
dress	skin	stop
glass	frog	sled
smell		

Alternate Words

clock	brick	drill
still	trap	crab
flag	twin	spot
step		

 **Offline** ⓯ minutes per day

Complete the Spelling activities with students. **For the full instructions for each activity, refer to pages SP 8–13.**

Day 1 ....

Introduce Heart Words and Beginning Blends

 **Materials**

- index cards (24)
- whiteboard (optional)

Advance Preparation

Write each Heart, Target, Challenge, and Alternate Word on a separate index card. Indicate on each card whether a word is a Heart, Target, Challenge, or Alternate Word.

Pretest

1. **Administer** a pretest using the Heart and Target Words.

2. **Gather** students' Words to Learn cards.

Note: If students didn't misspell any Heart, Target, Challenge, or Alternate Words, mark Lessons 2 and 3 complete and move to the online activity for Day 4 to practice for the Unit Checkpoint on Day 5.

Heart Words

⮊ *Skip this activity if students didn't misspell any Heart Words on this unit's pretest.*

1. **Gather** the Words to Learn cards for any Heart Words.

2. **Practice** the *new* Heart Words.

3. **Practice** *all* Heart Words.

4. **Track mastery** of Heart Words.

Target Words

⮊ *Skip this activity if students didn't misspell any Target Words on this unit's pretest.*

1. **Gather** the Words to Learn cards for any Target Words.

2. **Discover** the new spelling convention.

3. **Practice** the Target Words.

Challenge Words

↻ *Skip this activity if students are struggling with the Heart Words and Target Words.*

1. **Gather** the Words to Learn cards for any Challenge Words.
2. **Discover** the new spelling convention in the Challenge Words.
3. **Practice** the Challenge Words.

Alternate Words

↻ *Skip this activity if students don't have anyWords to Learn cards for Alternate Words.*

1. **Gather** the Words to Learn cards for any Alternate Words.
2. **Discover** the new spelling convention in the Alternate Words.
3. **Practice** the Alternate Words.

Day 2 ....

Practice Spelling Words
Practice using the Activity Bank.

Day 3 ....

Practice Spelling Words
Practice using the Activity Bank.

 **15 minutes**

Day 4 ....

Review Spelling Words
Review using the online activity.

Offline ⏱ 15 minutes

Day 5

Unit Checkpoint

1. **Dictate** the Heart Words and Target Words.

2. **Check** students' answers.

3. **Review** the words students misspelled.

Reward: If students scored 80 percent or above on the Unit Checkpoint, add a sticker to the Unit 8 box on students' My Accomplishments chart. If students scored under 80 percent, continue to practice the words that they missed and add a sticker to this unit once they have mastered the words.

Heart Words and Digraph Blends & Trigraphs

Target spelling convention – **blends containing consonant _n_ + digraph _ch_; the single sound made by the letter combination _tch_**

In a digraph, two letters combine to make one sound. In a trigraph, three letters combine to make one sound. Some of this unit's spelling words contain a digraph blend, which blends the consonant _n_ and the digraph _ch_. The rest of this unit's words contain the trigraph _tch_, which makes the sound /ch/. To spell a word with a digraph blend or a trigraph, we have to listen carefully to the sounds in the word.

Objectives
- Spell Heart Words.
- Spell words containing a digraph blend.
- Spell words containing the trigraph _tch_.

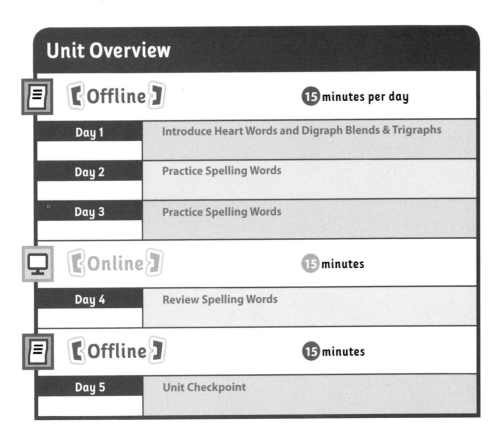

Unit Overview

📋 『Offline』 🕐15 minutes per day

Day 1	Introduce Heart Words and Digraph Blends & Trigraphs
Day 2	Practice Spelling Words
Day 3	Practice Spelling Words

🖥 『Online』 🕐15 minutes

| Day 4 | Review Spelling Words |

📋 『Offline』 🕐15 minutes

| Day 5 | Unit Checkpoint |

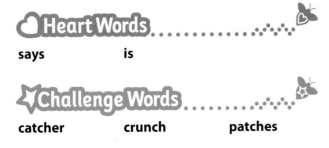

☁ Heart Words ....

| says | is |

★ Challenge Words ....

| catcher | crunch | patches |

◎ Target Words ....

pitch	ranch	catch
bench	itch	hatch
lunch	fetch	switch
pinch		

Alternate Words ....

munch	twitch	ditch
sketch	finch	punch
batch	match	bunch
stitch		

Offline 🕐 **minutes per day**

Complete the Spelling activities with students. **For the full instructions for each activity, refer to pages SP 8–13.**

Day 1 ....

Introduce Heart Words and Digraph Blends & Trigraphs

Materials

- index cards (25)
- whiteboard (optional)

Advance Preparation

Write each Heart, Target, Challenge, and Alternate Word on a separate index card. Indicate on each card whether a word is a Heart, Target, Challenge, or Alternate Word.

Pretest

1. **Administer** a pretest using the Heart and Target Words.

2. **Gather** students' Words to Learn cards.

Note: If students didn't misspell any Heart, Target, Challenge, or Alternate Words, mark Lessons 2 and 3 complete and move to the online activity for Day 4 to practice for the Unit Checkpoint on Day 5.

Heart Words

➲ *Skip this activity if students didn't misspell any Heart Words on this unit's pretest.*

1. **Gather** the Words to Learn cards for any Heart Words.

2. **Practice** the *new* Heart Words.

3. **Practice** *all* Heart Words.

4. **Track mastery** of Heart Words.

Target Words

➲ *Skip this activity if students didn't misspell any Target Words on this unit's pretest.*

1. **Gather** the Words to Learn cards for any Target Words.

2. **Discover** the new spelling convention.

3. **Practice** the Target Words.

Challenge Words

↪ *Skip this activity if students are struggling with the Heart Words and Target Words.*

1. **Gather** the Words to Learn cards for any Challenge Words.
2. **Discover** the new spelling convention in the Challenge Words.
3. **Practice** the Challenge Words.

Alternate Words

↪ *Skip this activity if students don't have any Words to Learn cards for Alternate Words.*

1. **Gather** the Words to Learn cards for any Alternate Words.
2. **Discover** the new spelling convention in the Alternate Words.
3. **Practice** the Alternate Words.

Day 2

Practice Spelling Words

Practice using the Activity Bank.

Day 3

Practice Spelling Words

Practice using the Activity Bank.

 **15 minutes**

Day 4

Review Spelling Words

Review using the online activity.

[Offline] 15 minutes

Day 5

Unit Checkpoint

1. **Dictate** the Heart Words and Target Words.

2. **Check** students' answers.

3. **Review** the words students misspelled.

Reward: If students scored 80 percent or above on the Unit Checkpoint, add a sticker to the Unit 9 box on students' My Accomplishments chart. If students scored under 80 percent, continue to practice the words that they missed and add a sticker to this unit once they have mastered the words.

Heart Words and Oddball Sounds

Target spelling convention – **words ending in *–ang*, *–ing*, *–ong*, and *–ung*; words ending in *–ank*, *–ink*, *–onk*, and *–unk***

Each of the following endings makes its own sound: *–ang*, *–ing*, *–ong*, *–ung*, *–ank*, *–ink*, *–onk*, and *–unk*. When spelling words that contain these endings, listen carefully to identify the correct ending sound. This unit's words end in *–ang*, *–ing*, *–ong*, *–ung*, *–ank*, *–ink*, *–onk*, or *–unk*.

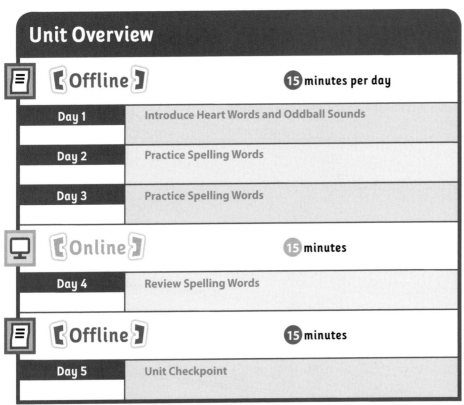

Unit Overview

Offline — 15 minutes per day

Day 1	Introduce Heart Words and Oddball Sounds
Day 2	Practice Spelling Words
Day 3	Practice Spelling Words

Online — 15 minutes

| Day 4 | Review Spelling Words |

Offline — 15 minutes

| Day 5 | Unit Checkpoint |

Heart Words

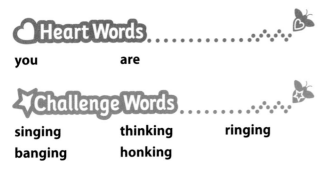

you   are

Challenge Words

singing   thinking   ringing

banging   honking

Target Words

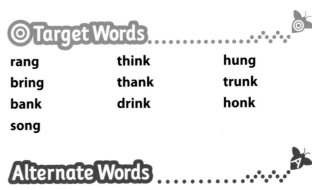

rang	think	hung
bring	thank	trunk
bank	drink	honk
song		

Alternate Words

chunk	drank	skunk
junk	sing	long
swing	hang	pink
tank		

 Offline 🕔 **minutes per day**

Complete the Spelling activities with students. **For the full instructions for each activity, refer to pages SP 8–13.**

Day 1

Introduce Heart Words and Oddball Sounds

Materials

- index cards (27)
- whiteboard (optional)

Advance Preparation

Write each Heart, Target, Challenge, and Alternate Word on a separate index card. Indicate on each card whether a word is a Heart, Target, Challenge, or Alternate Word.

Pretest

1. **Administer** a pretest using the Heart and Target Words.

2. **Gather** students' Words to Learn cards.

Note: If students didn't misspell any Heart, Target, Challenge, or Alternate Words, mark Lessons 2 and 3 complete and move to the online activity for Day 4 to practice for the Unit Checkpoint on Day 5.

Heart Words

⮑ *Skip this activity if students didn't misspell any Heart Words on this unit's pretest.*

1. **Gather** the Words to Learn cards for any Heart Words.

2. **Practice** the *new* Heart Words.

3. **Practice** *all* Heart Words.

4. **Track mastery** of Heart Words.

Target Words

⮑ *Skip this activity if students didn't misspell any Target Words on this unit's pretest.*

1. **Gather** the Words to Learn cards for any Target Words.

2. **Discover** the new spelling convention.

3. **Practice** the Target Words.

Challenge Words

⮥ *Skip this activity if students are struggling with the Heart Words and Target Words.*

1. **Gather** the Words to Learn cards for any Challenge Words.
2. **Discover** the new spelling convention in the Challenge Words.
3. **Practice** the Challenge Words.

Alternate Words

⮥ *Skip this activity if students don't have any Words to Learn cards for Alternate Words.*

1. **Gather** the Words to Learn cards for any Alternate Words.
2. **Discover** the new spelling convention in the Alternate Words.
3. **Practice** the Alternate Words.

Day 2 ··

Practice Spelling Words

Practice using the Activity Bank.

Day 3 ··

Practice Spelling Words

Practice using the Activity Bank.

 **15 minutes**

Day 4 ··

Review Spelling Words

Review using the online activity.

[Offline] 15 minutes

Day 5

Unit Checkpoint

1. **Dictate** the Heart Words and Target Words.

2. **Check** students' answers.

3. **Review** the words students misspelled.

Reward: If students scored 80 percent or above on the Unit Checkpoint, add a sticker to the Unit 10 box on students' My Accomplishments chart. If students scored under 80 percent, continue to practice the words that they missed and add a sticker to this unit once they have mastered the words.

Heart Words and the Sound /kw/ Spelled *qu*

Target spelling convention – **creating the /kw/ sound with the letters *qu***

In the English language, the letter *q* is almost always followed by the letter *u*. We can remember this rule by saying, "Q and *u* stick together like glue." We even call *q* and *u* "glue letters." The letters *qu* make the sound /kw/. However, the *u* does not act like a vowel when it is with *q*. That's why *qu* is almost always followed by a vowel. This unit's words all contain the letters *qu*.

Objectives
- Spell Heart Words.
- Spell words containing the letter combination *qu*.

Unit Overview

Offline		**15** minutes per day
Day 1	Introduce Heart Words and the Sound /kw/ Spelled *qu*	
Day 2	Practice Spelling Words	
Day 3	Practice Spelling Words	
Online		**15** minutes
Day 4	Review Spelling Words	
Offline		**15** minutes
Day 5	Unit Checkpoint	

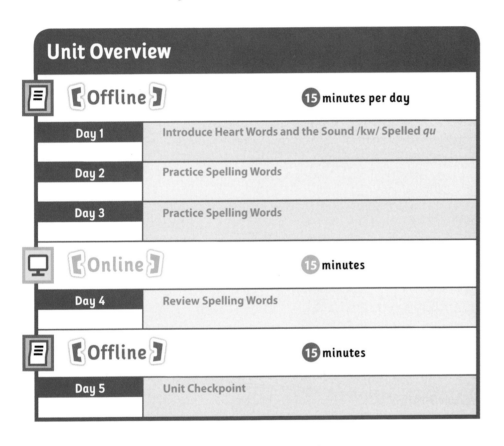

♥ Heart Words

your	who	where

◎ Target Words

quit	squish	squint
quilt	squid	quack
quiz	quill	quick

☆ Challenge Words

quilting	squishing	quacking

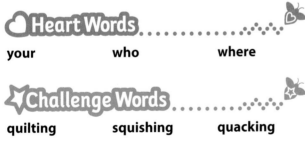

Alternate Words

quirk	squash	squirt
squall	squirm	

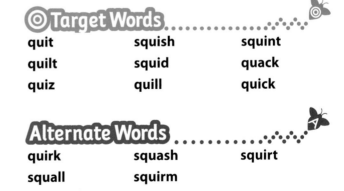

 **15 minutes per day**

Complete the Spelling activities with students. **For the full instructions for each activity, refer to pages SP 8–13.**

Day 1

Introduce Heart Words and the Sound /kw/ Spelled *qu*

* index cards (20)
* whiteboard (optional)

Advance Preparation

Write each Heart, Target, Challenge, and Alternate Word on a separate index card. Indicate on each card whether a word is a Heart, Target, Challenge, or Alternate Word.

Pretest

1. **Administer** a pretest using the Heart and Target Words.

2. **Gather** students' Words to Learn cards.

Note: If students didn't misspell any Heart, Target, Challenge, or Alternate Words, mark Lessons 2 and 3 complete and move to the online activity for Day 4 to practice for the Unit Checkpoint on Day 5.

Heart Words

⟳ *Skip this activity if students didn't misspell any Heart Words on this unit's pretest.*

1. **Gather** the Words to Learn cards for any Heart Words.

2. **Practice** the *new* Heart Words.

3. **Practice** *all* Heart Words.

4. **Track mastery** of Heart Words.

Target Words

⟳ *Skip this activity if students didn't misspell any Target Words on this unit's pretest.*

1. **Gather** the Words to Learn cards for any Target Words.

2. **Discover** the new spelling convention.

3. **Practice** the Target Words.

Challenge Words

➲ *Skip this activity if students are struggling with the Heart Words and Target Words.*

1. **Gather** the Words to Learn cards for any Challenge Words.
2. **Discover** the new spelling convention in the Challenge Words.
3. **Practice** the Challenge Words.

Alternate Words

➲ *Skip this activity if students don't have any Words to Learn cards for Alternate Words.*

1. **Gather** the Words to Learn cards for any Alternate Words.
2. **Discover** the new spelling convention in the Alternate Words.
3. **Practice** the Alternate Words.

Day 2 ....

Practice Spelling Words

Practice using the Activity Bank.

Day 3 ....

Practice Spelling Words

Practice using the Activity Bank.

 **15** minutes

Day 4 ....

Review Spelling Words

Review using the online activity.

[Offline] ⑮ minutes

Unit Checkpoint

1. **Dictate** the Heart Words and Target Words.

2. **Check** students' answers.

3. **Review** the words students misspelled.

Reward: If students scored 80 percent or above on the Unit Checkpoint, add a sticker to the Unit 11 box on students' My Accomplishments chart. If students scored under 80 percent, continue to practice the words that they missed and add a sticker to this unit once they have mastered the words.

Heart Words and Triple Consonant Blends

Target spelling convention – **blends containing three consonants**

In a triple consonant blend, three consonants combine, but each consonant makes its own sound. To spell a word with a triple consonant blend, listen carefully to the three sounds in the blend. This unit's words all begin with a triple consonant blend and have a short vowel.

Objectives
- Spell Heart Words.
- Spell words containing triple consonant blends.

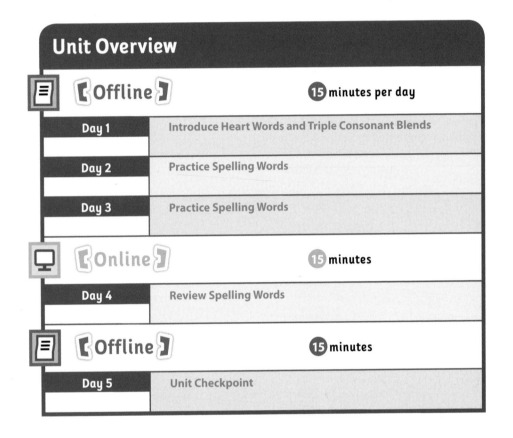

Unit Overview

Offline — 15 minutes per day

Day 1	Introduce Heart Words and Triple Consonant Blends
Day 2	Practice Spelling Words
Day 3	Practice Spelling Words

Online — 15 minutes

| Day 4 | Review Spelling Words |

Offline — 15 minutes

| Day 5 | Unit Checkpoint |

♡ Heart Words

one   once

☆ Challenge Words

splendid

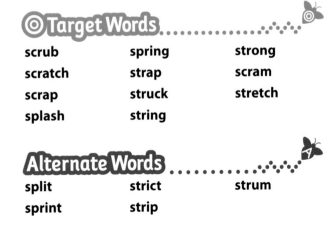

◎ Target Words

scrub	spring	strong
scratch	strap	scram
scrap	struck	stretch
splash	string	

Alternate Words

| split | strict | strum |
| sprint | strip | |

 **⏱ 15 minutes per day**

Complete the Spelling activities with students. **For the full instructions for each activity, refer to pages SP 8–13.**

Day 1 ....

Introduce Heart Words and Triple Consonant Blends

Materials

- index cards (19)
- whiteboard (optional)

Advance Preparation

Write each Heart, Target, Challenge, and Alternate Word on a separate index card. Indicate on each card whether a word is a Heart, Target, Challenge, or Alternate Word.

Pretest

1. **Administer** a pretest using the Heart and Target Words.
2. **Gather** students' Words to Learn cards.

Note: If students didn't misspell any Heart, Target, Challenge, or Alternate Words, mark Lessons 2 and 3 complete and move to the online activity for Day 4 to practice for the Unit Checkpoint on Day 5.

Heart Words

➲ *Skip this activity if students didn't misspell any Heart Words on this unit's pretest.*

1. **Gather** the Words to Learn cards for any Heart Words.
2. **Practice** the *new* Heart Words.
3. **Practice** *all* Heart Words.
4. **Track mastery** of Heart Words.

Target Words

➲ *Skip this activity if students didn't misspell any Target Words on this unit's pretest.*

1. **Gather** the Words to Learn cards for any Target Words.
2. **Discover** the new spelling convention.
3. **Practice** the Target Words.

Challenge Words

⊃ *Skip this activity if students are struggling with the Heart Words and Target Words.*

1. **Gather** the Words to Learn cards for any Challenge Words.
2. **Discover** the new spelling convention in the Challenge Words.
3. **Practice** the Challenge Words.

Alternate Words

⊃ *Skip this activity if students don't have any Words to Learn cards for Alternate Words.*

1. **Gather** the Words to Learn cards for any Alternate Words.
2. **Discover** the new spelling convention in the Alternate Words.
3. **Practice** the Alternate Words.

Day 2 ···

Practice Spelling Words

Practice using the Activity Bank.

Day 3 ···

Practice Spelling Words

Practice using the Activity Bank.

 **15** minutes

Day 4 ···

Review Spelling Words

Review using the online activity.

⟦Offline⟧ **15** minutes

Unit Checkpoint

1. **Dictate** the Heart Words and Target Words.

2. **Check** students' answers.

3. **Review** the words students misspelled.

Reward: If students scored 80 percent or above on the Unit Checkpoint, add a sticker to the Unit 12 box on students' My Accomplishments chart. If students scored under 80 percent, continue to practice the words that they missed and add a sticker to this unit once they have mastered the words.

Heart Words and Long *a* & *i* Spelled with a Silent *e*

Target spelling convention — **long *a* or *i* + consonant + silent *e***

When a letter makes no sound in a word, we say that the letter is silent. Now we're going to learn to spell words containing a silent *e*. When a word has a vowel followed by a consonant and then an *e*, the vowel sound is usually long and the *e* is silent. This unit's words all have a long *a* or a long *i* and a silent *e*.

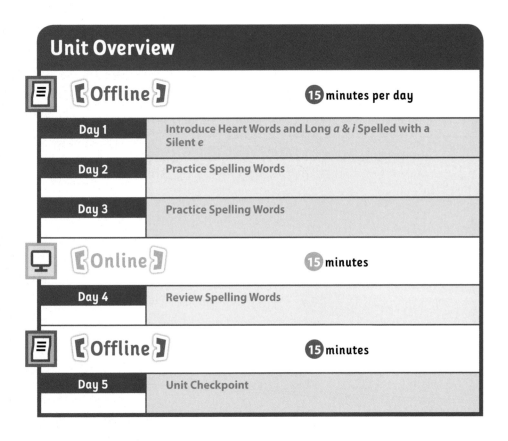

Unit Overview

📄 **〖Offline〗**		ⓕ minutes per day
Day 1	Introduce Heart Words and Long *a* & *i* Spelled with a Silent *e*	
Day 2	Practice Spelling Words	
Day 3	Practice Spelling Words	

🖥 **〖Online〗**		ⓕ minutes
Day 4	Review Spelling Words	

📄 **〖Offline〗**		ⓕ minutes
Day 5	Unit Checkpoint	

♡ Heart Words
goes	does

☆ Challenge Words
became	sometimes	beside

◎ Target Words
bite	shake	time
gave	like	made
fine	take	save
make	state	white

Alternate Words
game	cave	dive
shade	gate	bake
dime	bike	kite
rake		

[Offline] ⏱ **15 minutes per day**

Complete the Spelling activities with students. **For the full instructions for each activity, refer to pages SP8–13.**

Introduce Heart Words and Long *a* & *i* Spelled with a Silent *e*

[Materials]

- index cards (27)
- whiteboard (optional)

Advance Preparation

Write each Heart, Target, Challenge, and Alternate Word on a separate index card. Indicate on each card whether a word is a Heart, Target, Challenge, or Alternate Word.

Pretest

1. **Administer** a pretest using the Heart and Target Words.
2. **Gather** students' Words to Learn cards.

Note: If students didn't misspell any Heart, Target, Challenge, or Alternate Words, mark Lessons 2 and 3 complete and move to the online activity for Day 4 to practice for the Unit Checkpoint on Day 5.

Heart Words

↻ *Skip this activity if students didn't misspell any Heart Words on this unit's pretest.*

1. **Gather** the Words to Learn cards for any Heart Words.
2. **Practice** the *new* Heart Words.
3. **Practice** *all* Heart Words.
4. **Track mastery** of Heart Words.

Target Words

↻ *Skip this activity if students didn't misspell any Target Words on this unit's pretest.*

1. **Gather** the Words to Learn cards for any Target Words.
2. **Discover** the new spelling convention.
3. **Practice** the Target Words.

Challenge Words

➲ *Skip this activity if students are struggling with the Heart Words and Target Words.*

1. **Gather** the Words to Learn cards for any Challenge Words.
2. **Discover** the new spelling convention in the Challenge Words.
3. **Practice** the Challenge Words.

Alternate Words

➲ *Skip this activity if students don't have any Words to Learn cards for Alternate Words.*

1. **Gather** the Words to Learn cards for any Alternate Words.
2. **Discover** the new spelling convention in the Alternate Words.
3. **Practice** the Alternate Words.

Day 2

Practice Spelling Words

Practice using the Activity Bank.

Day 3

Practice Spelling Words

Practice using the Activity Bank.

 **15** minutes

Day 4

Review Spelling Words

Review using the online activity.

Day 5

Unit Checkpoint

1. **Dictate** the Heart Words and Target Words.

2. **Check** students' answers.

3. **Review** the words students misspelled.

Reward: If students scored 80 percent or above on the Unit Checkpoint, add a sticker to the Unit 13 box on students' My Accomplishments chart. If students scored under 80 percent, continue to practice the words that they missed and add a sticker to this unit once they have mastered the words.

Heart Words and Long *e*, *o*, & *u* Spelled with a Silent *e*

Target spelling convention — **long *e*, *o*, or *u* + consonant + silent *e***

When a word has an *e*, an *o*, or a *u* followed by a consonant and then an *e*, the vowel sound is usually long and the *e* is silent. This unit's words all have a long *e*, a long *o*, or a long *u* and a silent *e*.

Objectives
- Spell Heart Words.
- Spell words containing a long vowel sound and ending with silent *e*.

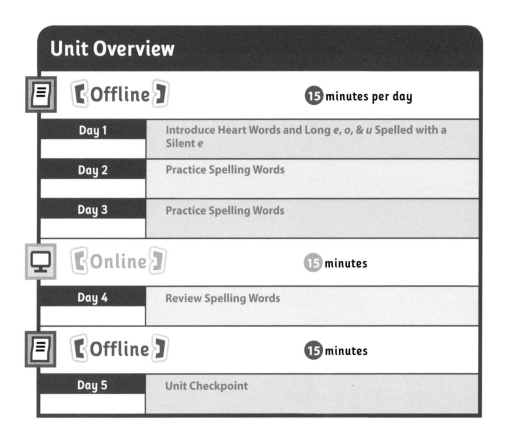

Unit Overview

Offline — 15 minutes per day

Day 1	Introduce Heart Words and Long *e*, *o*, & *u* Spelled with a Silent *e*
Day 2	Practice Spelling Words
Day 3	Practice Spelling Words

Online — 15 minutes

| Day 4 | Review Spelling Words |

Offline — 15 minutes

| Day 5 | Unit Checkpoint |

Heart Words

because

Challenge Words

alone   homesick   bathrobe

Target Words

these	stroke	tune
eve	huge	June
stone	use	fuse
drove	cute	flute

Alternate Words

theme	hole	code
broke	tote	rode
those	mute	slope
quote		

 **minutes per day**

Complete the Spelling activities with students. **For the full instructions for each activity, refer to pages SP 8–13.**

Day 1

Introduce Heart Words and Long *e*, *o*, & *u* Spelled with a Silent *e*

Materials

- index cards (26)
- whiteboard (optional)

Advance Preparation

Write each Heart, Target, Challenge, and Alternate Word on a separate index card. Indicate on each card whether a word is a Heart, Target, Challenge, or Alternate Word.

Pretest

1. **Administer** a pretest using the Heart and Target Words.

2. **Gather** students' Words to Learn cards.

Note: If students didn't misspell any Heart, Target, Challenge, or Alternate Words, mark Lessons 2 and 3 complete and move to the online activity for Day 4 to practice for the Unit Checkpoint on Day 5.

Heart Words

⮌ *Skip this activity if students didn't misspell any Heart Words on this unit's pretest.*

1. **Gather** the Words to Learn cards for any Heart Words.

2. **Practice** the *new* Heart Words.

3. **Practice** *all* Heart Words.

4. **Track mastery** of Heart Words.

Target Words

⮌ *Skip this activity if students didn't misspell any Target Words on this unit's pretest.*

1. **Gather** the Words to Learn cards for any Target Words.

2. **Discover** the new spelling convention.

3. **Practice** the Target Words.

Challenge Words

⮌ *Skip this activity if students are struggling with the Heart Words and Target Words.*

1. **Gather** the Words to Learn cards for any Challenge Words.
2. **Discover** the new spelling convention in the Challenge Words.
3. **Practice** the Challenge Words.

Alternate Words

⮌ *Skip this activity if students don't have any Words to Learn cards for Alternate Words.*

1. **Gather** the Words to Learn cards for any Alternate Words.
2. **Discover** the new spelling convention in the Alternate Words.
3. **Practice** the Alternate Words.

Day 2

Practice Spelling Words

Practice using the Activity Bank.

Day 3

Practice Spelling Words

Practice using the Activity Bank.

 **15** minutes

Day 4

Review Spelling Words

Review using the online activity.

Offline ⑮ minutes

Unit Checkpoint

1. **Dictate** the Heart Words and Target Words.

2. **Check** students' answers.

3. **Review** the words students misspelled.

Reward: If students scored 80 percent or above on the Unit Checkpoint, add a sticker to the Unit 14 box on students' My Accomplishments chart. If students scored under 80 percent, continue to practice the words that they missed and add a sticker to this unit once they have mastered the words.

Heart Words and Short Vowel Sounds with a Silent *e*

Target spelling convention – **short vowel sound + consonant + silent *e***

All of this unit's words end with the silent *e*. However, they do not contain the long vowel sound. Instead, the vowel sounds in this unit's words are short.

Objectives

* Spell Heart Words.
* Spell words containing a short vowel sound and ending with silent *e*.

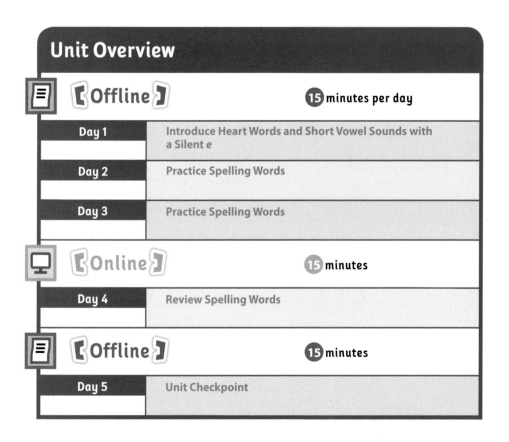

Unit Overview

⟦Offline⟧   **15** minutes per day

Day 1	Introduce Heart Words and Short Vowel Sounds with a Silent *e*
Day 2	Practice Spelling Words
Day 3	Practice Spelling Words

⟦Online⟧   **15** minutes

| Day 4 | Review Spelling Words |

⟦Offline⟧   **15** minutes

| Day 5 | Unit Checkpoint |

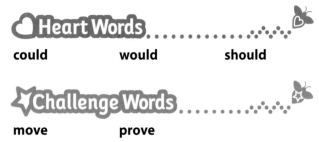

Heart Words

| could | would | should |

Challenge Words

| move | prove |

Target Words

give	none	done
love	glove	shove
come	have	some
live		

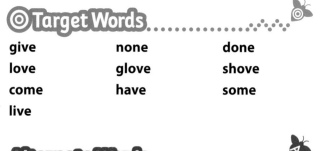

Alternate Words

| above | active | olive |
| dove | festive | |

 **Offline** 🕐 minutes per day

Complete the Spelling activities with students. **For the full instructions for each activity, refer to pages SP 8–13.**

Day 1 ....

Introduce Heart Words and Short Vowel Sounds with a Silent *e*

Materials

- index cards (20)
- whiteboard (optional)

Advance Preparation

Write each Heart, Target, Challenge, and Alternate Word on a separate index card. Indicate on each card whether a word is a Heart, Target, Challenge, or Alternate Word.

Pretest

1. **Administer** a pretest using the Heart and Target Words.

2. **Gather** students' Words to Learn cards.

Note: If students didn't misspell any Heart, Target, Challenge, or Alternate Words, mark Lessons 2 and 3 complete and move to the online activity for Day 4 to practice for the Unit Checkpoint on Day 5.

Heart Words

➲ *Skip this activity if students didn't misspell any Heart Words on this unit's pretest.*

1. **Gather** the Words to Learn cards for any Heart Words.

2. **Practice** the *new* Heart Words.

3. **Practice** *all* Heart Words.

4. **Track mastery** of Heart Words.

Target Words

➲ *Skip this activity if students didn't misspell any Target Words on this unit's pretest.*

1. **Gather** the Words to Learn cards for any Target Words.

2. **Discover** the new spelling convention.

3. **Practice** the Target Words.

Challenge Words

⮑ *Skip this activity if students are struggling with the Heart Words and Target Words.*

1. **Gather** the Words to Learn cards for any Challenge Words.
2. **Discover** the new spelling convention in the Challenge Words.
3. **Practice** the Challenge Words.

Alternate Words

⮑ *Skip this activity if students don't have any Words to Learn cards for Alternate Words.*

1. **Gather** the Words to Learn cards for any Alternate Words.
2. **Discover** the new spelling convention in the Alternate Words.
3. **Practice** the Alternate Words.

Day 2 ....

Practice Spelling Words

Practice using the Activity Bank.

Day 3 ....

Practice Spelling Words

Practice using the Activity Bank.

 **minutes**

Day 4 ....

Review Spelling Words

Review using the online activity.

 **[Offline]** ⑮ minutes

Unit Checkpoint

1. **Dictate** the Heart Words and Target Words.

2. **Check** students' answers.

3. **Review** the words students misspelled.

 Reward: If students scored 80 percent or above on the Unit Checkpoint, add a sticker to the Unit 15 box on students' My Accomplishments chart. If students scored under 80 percent, continue to practice the words that they missed and add a sticker to this unit once they have mastered the words.

Heart Words and the Ending *–ed*

Target spelling convention – two consonants + the suffix *–ed*

We can add the suffix *–ed* to an action word ending in two or more consonants without changing the spelling of the base word. The suffix *–ed* can be pronounced /ed/, /t/, or /d/. This unit's words all end with the suffix *–ed*.

Objectives

- Spell Heart Words.
- Spell words with the ending *–ed*.

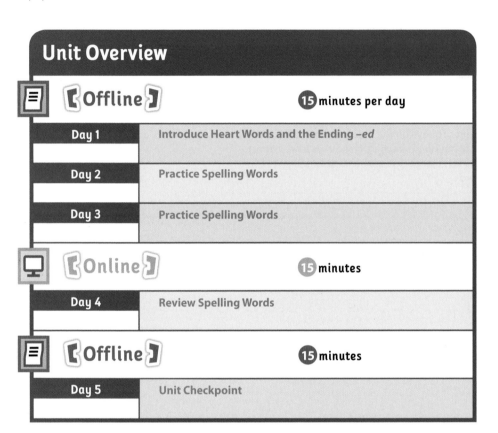

Unit Overview

Offline	15 minutes per day
Day 1	Introduce Heart Words and the Ending *–ed*
Day 2	Practice Spelling Words
Day 3	Practice Spelling Words
Online	15 minutes
Day 4	Review Spelling Words
Offline	15 minutes
Day 5	Unit Checkpoint

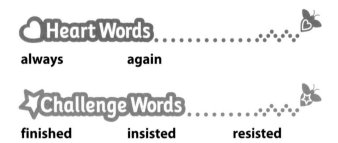

Heart Words

always **again**

Challenge Words

finished **insisted** **resisted**

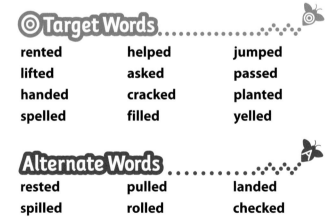

Target Words

rented	helped	jumped
lifted	asked	passed
handed	cracked	planted
spelled	filled	yelled

Alternate Words

rested	pulled	landed
spilled	rolled	checked

 **⏱ 15 minutes per day**

Complete the Spelling activities with students. **For the full instructions for each activity, refer to pages SP 8–13.**

Day 1 ....

Introduce Heart Words and the Ending –ed

- index cards (23)
- whiteboard (optional)

Advance Preparation

Write each Heart, Target, Challenge, and Alternate Word on a separate index card. Indicate on each card whether a word is a Heart, Target, Challenge, or Alternate Word.

Pretest

1. **Administer** a pretest using the Heart and Target Words.

2. **Gather** students' Words to Learn cards.

Note: If students didn't misspell any Heart, Target, Challenge, or Alternate Words, mark Lessons 2 and 3 complete and move to the online activity for Day 4 to practice for the Unit Checkpoint on Day 5.

Heart Words

➲ *Skip this activity if students didn't misspell any Heart Words on this unit's pretest.*

1. **Gather** the Words to Learn cards for any Heart Words.

2. **Practice** the *new* Heart Words.

3. **Practice** *all* Heart Words.

4. **Track mastery** of Heart Words.

Target Words

➲ *Skip this activity if students didn't misspell any Target Words on this unit's pretest.*

1. **Gather** the Words to Learn cards for any Target Words.

2. **Discover** the new spelling convention.

3. **Practice** the Target Words.

Challenge Words

↩ *Skip this activity if students are struggling with the Heart Words and Target Words.*

1. **Gather** the Words to Learn cards for any Challenge Words.
2. **Discover** the new spelling convention in the Challenge Words.
3. **Practice** the Challenge Words.

Alternate Words

↩ *Skip this activity if students don't have any Words to Learn cards for Alternate Words.*

1. **Gather** the Words to Learn cards for any Alternate Words.
2. **Discover** the new spelling convention in the Alternate Words.
3. **Practice** the Alternate Words.

Day 2 •

Practice Spelling Words

Practice using the Activity Bank.

Day 3 •

Practice Spelling Words

Practice using the Activity Bank.

 **15 minutes**

Day 4 •

Review Spelling Words

Review using the online activity.

Day 5

Unit Checkpoint

1. **Dictate** the Heart Words and Target Words.

2. **Check** students' answers.

3. **Review** the words students misspelled.

Reward: If students scored 80 percent or above on the Unit Checkpoint, add a sticker to the Unit 16 box on students' My Accomplishments chart. If students scored under 80 percent, continue to practice the words that they missed and add a sticker to this unit once they have mastered the words.

Heart Words and Doubling Consonants When Adding *–ing* & *–ed*

Target spelling convention – short vowel + consonant + the suffixes *–ing* and *–ed*

When we add *–ing* or *–ed* to a word that ends with a short vowel followed by a consonant, we double the final consonant before adding *–ing* or *–ed*. This unit's words all have a doubled consonant and the ending *–ed* or *–ing*.

Objectives
- Spell Heart Words.
- Spell words requiring a doubled consonant before the endings *–ed* or *–ing*.

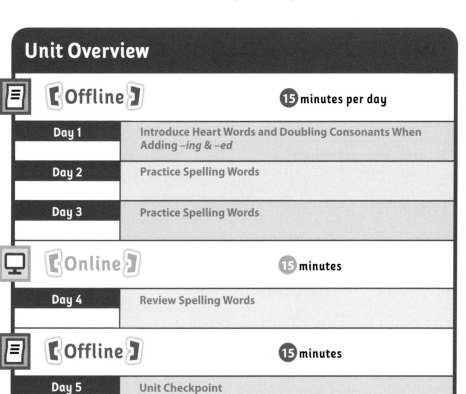

Unit Overview

Offline — 15 minutes per day

Day 1	Introduce Heart Words and Doubling Consonants When Adding *–ing* & *–ed*
Day 2	Practice Spelling Words
Day 3	Practice Spelling Words

Online — 15 minutes

| Day 4 | Review Spelling Words |

Offline — 15 minutes

| Day 5 | Unit Checkpoint |

Heart Words
other	mother	brother
father		

Challenge Words
rewrapping	uncapped	programmed

Target Words
shopping	swimming	dimmed
batting	getting	rubbed
quitting	patted	digging
running	stopped	planned

Alternate Words
sunning	stopping	wagging
flopped	hummed	grabbed
planning	slapping	tripped
slipped		

[Offline] ⓘ **minutes per day**

Complete the Spelling activities with students. **For the full instructions for each activity, refer to pages SP 8–13.**

Day 1 ....

Introduce Heart Words and Doubling Consonants When Adding *–ing* & *–ed*

[Materials]

- index cards (29)
- whiteboard (optional)

Advance Preparation

Write each Heart, Target, Challenge, and Alternate Word on a separate index card. Indicate on each card whether a word is a Heart, Target, Challenge, or Alternate Word.

Pretest

1. **Administer** a pretest using the Heart and Target Words.

2. **Gather** students' Words to Learn cards.

Note: If students didn't misspell any Heart, Target, Challenge, or Alternate Words, mark Lessons 2 and 3 complete and move to the online activity for Day 4 to practice for the Unit Checkpoint on Day 5.

Heart Words

⮑ *Skip this activity if students didn't misspell any Heart Words on this unit's pretest.*

1. **Gather** the Words to Learn cards for any Heart Words.

2. **Practice** the *new* Heart Words.

3. **Practice** *all* Heart Words.

4. **Track mastery** of Heart Words.

Target Words

⮑ *Skip this activity if students didn't misspell any Target Words on this unit's pretest.*

1. **Gather** the Words to Learn cards for any Target Words.

2. **Discover** the new spelling convention.

3. **Practice** the Target Words.

Challenge Words

⤺ *Skip this activity if students are struggling with the Heart Words and Target Words.*

1. **Gather** the Words to Learn cards for any Challenge Words.
2. **Discover** the new spelling convention in the Challenge Words.
3. **Practice** the Challenge Words.

Alternate Words

⤺ *Skip this activity if students don't have any Words to Learn cards for Alternate Words.*

1. **Gather** the Words to Learn cards for any Alternate Words.
2. **Discover** the new spelling convention in the Alternate Words.
3. **Practice** the Alternate Words.

Day 2

Practice Spelling Words

Practice using the Activity Bank.

Day 3

Practice Spelling Words

Practice using the Activity Bank.

 **15 minutes**

Day 4

Review Spelling Words

Review using the online activity.

 **15** minutes

Unit Checkpoint

1. **Dictate** the Heart Words and Target Words.

2. **Check** students' answers.

3. **Review** the words students misspelled.

 Reward: If students scored 80 percent or above on the Unit Checkpoint, add a sticker to the Unit 17 box on students' My Accomplishments chart. If students scored under 80 percent, continue to practice the words that they missed and add a sticker to this unit once they have mastered the words.

Review Heart Words and Spelling Conventions

In this unit, students will review the Heart Words and spelling conventions they studied this semester. Refer to the Unit Plans of previous units for a detailed description of each spelling convention.

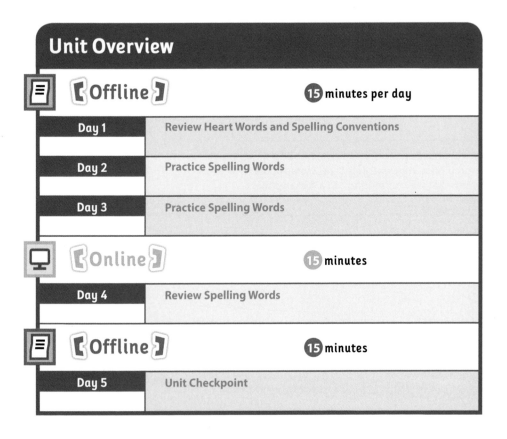

Unit Overview

Offline — 15 minutes per day

Day 1	Review Heart Words and Spelling Conventions
Day 2	Practice Spelling Words
Day 3	Practice Spelling Words

Online — 15 minutes

| Day 4 | Review Spelling Words |

Offline — 15 minutes

| Day 5 | Unit Checkpoint |

Objectives
- Spell Heart Words.
- Spell CVC words.
- Spell words ending with double letters.
- Spell words ending in the digraph *ck*.
- Spell plurals.
- Spell words containing the digraph *th*.
- Spell words containing the digraph *wh*.
- Spell words containing the digraph *sh*.
- Spell words containing the digraph *ch*.
- Spell words ending in a consonant blend.
- Spell words beginning with a consonant blend.
- Spell words containing a digraph blend.
- Spell words containing the trigraph *tch*.
- Spell words ending in –*ang*, –*ing*, –*ong*, or –*ung*.
- Spell words ending in –*ank*, –*ink*, –*onk*, or –*unk*.
- Spell words containing the letter combination *qu*.
- Spell words containing triple consonant blends.
- Spell words containing a long vowel sound and ending with silent *e*.
- Spell words containing a short vowel sound and ending with silent *e*.
- Spell words with the ending –*ed*.
- Spell words requiring a doubled consonant before the endings –*ed* or –*ing*.

Heart Words
where	goes	because
said		

Challenge Words
whiplash	homesick	became

Target Words
man	shake	huge
will	black	give
bench	bank	rented
these	squish	shopping

Alternate Words
math	box	broke
sprint	kite	brick
chick	dime	

[Offline] **15** minutes per day

Complete the Spelling activities with students. **For the full instructions for each activity, refer to pages SP 8–13.**

Complete the Spelling activities with students. **For the full instructions for each activity, refer to pages SP 8–13.**

Day 1 ··

Review Heart Words and Spelling Conventions

[Materials]

• whiteboard (optional)

Advance Preparation

Gather the index cards you made previously for the Heart, Target, Challenge, and Alternate Words listed.

Pretest

1. **Administer** a pretest using the Heart and Target Words.

2. **Gather** students' Words to Learn cards.

Note: If students didn't misspell any Heart, Target, Challenge, or Alternate Words, mark Lessons 2 and 3 complete and move to the online activity for Day 4 to practice for the Unit Checkpoint on Day 5.

Heart Words

➲ *Skip this activity if students didn't misspell any Heart Words on this unit's pretest.*

1. **Gather** the Words to Learn cards for any Heart Words.

2. **Practice** the Heart Words.

3. **Track mastery** of Heart Words.

Target Words

➲ *Skip this activity if students didn't misspell any Target Words on this unit's pretest.*

1. **Gather** the Words to Learn cards for any Target Words.

2. **Discover** the previously studied spelling convention in each Target Word.

3. **Practice** the Target Words.

Challenge Words

⮑ *Skip this activity if students are struggling with the Heart Words and Target Words.*

1. **Gather** the Words to Learn cards for any Challenge Words.
2. **Discover** the previously studied spelling convention in each Challenge Word.
3. **Practice** the Challenge Words.

Alternate Words

⮑ *Skip this activity if students don't have any Words to Learn cards for Alternate Words.*

1. **Gather** the Words to Learn cards for any Alternate Words.
2. **Discover** the previously studied spelling convention in each Alternate Word.
3. **Practice** the Alternate Words.

Day 2 ⋯⋯⋯⋯⋯⋯⋯⋯⋯⋯⋯⋯⋯⋯⋯⋯⋯⋯⋯⋯⋯⋯

Practice Spelling Words

Practice using the Activity Bank.

Day 3 ⋯⋯⋯⋯⋯⋯⋯⋯⋯⋯⋯⋯⋯⋯⋯⋯⋯⋯⋯⋯⋯⋯

Practice Spelling Words

Practice using the Activity Bank.

 ⑮ **minutes**

Day 4 ⋯⋯⋯⋯⋯⋯⋯⋯⋯⋯⋯⋯⋯⋯⋯⋯⋯⋯⋯⋯⋯⋯

Review Spelling Words

Review using the online activity.

 **15 minutes**

Unit Checkpoint

1. **Dictate** the Heart Words and Target Words.

2. **Check** students' answers.

3. **Review** the words students misspelled.

Rewards:

- If students scored 80 percent or above on the Unit Checkpoint, add a sticker to the Unit 18 box on students' My Accomplishments chart. If students scored under 80 percent, continue to practice the words that they missed and add a sticker to this unit once they have mastered the words.

- Help students find and play the online Spelling game, Spell 'n Stack. Students should use level 1.

Spelling Activity Bank

Word Train

1. Say each of the Words to Learn to students.

2. Have students write each word end-to-end as one long word, using different colors of crayon or ink for different words.

3. Note any words that students spelled incorrectly, and correct the spelling errors with students.

Vowel-Free Words

1. Say each of the Words to Learn to students. Have students write only the consonants in the word and put a dot where each vowel belongs.

2. Have students tell you which vowel belongs where they placed each dot.

3. Note any words that students spelled incorrectly, and correct the spelling errors with students.

Fill In the Blank

1. Write a sentence that uses one of the Words to Learn, but leave a blank space where that word would go in the sentence.

2. Ask students to fill in the word that completes the sentence. Sometimes more than one word will correctly complete a sentence.

3. Repeat with each of the Words to Learn.

4. Note any words that students spelled incorrectly, and correct the spelling errors with students.

Silly Sentences

1. Ask students to write a silly sentence using each of the Words to Learn.

2. Have students underline the word in each of their sentences.
   Sample sentence: *The dog was driving a car.*

3. Note any words that students spelled incorrectly, and correct the spelling errors with students.

Spelling Baseball

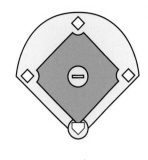

1. Draw a baseball diamond with four bases (see example).

2. Tell students that you are the pitcher and they are the batters.

3. Choose a word from the Words to Learn and ask students to spell it.

   ▸ If students spell the word correctly, they get to move one base.
   ▸ If the students spell the word incorrectly, that is one strike.
   ▸ If students get three strikes on the same word, that is one out.
   ▸ If students spell four words correctly, they have moved around all four bases. They score a run (one point)!

4. Continue giving students words until each of the Words to Learn has been used. See how many points students can earn.

Spelling Story

Have students write a very short story using as many of the Words to Learn as they can.

Colorful Words

1. Have students write each of the Words to Learn using two colors: one color for vowels and another color for consonants.

2. Note any words that students spelled incorrectly, and correct the spelling errors with students.

Materials

• crayons

Which Is Correct?

1. Write out three versions of one of the Words to Learn, spelling two versions incorrectly and one correctly.

2. Say the word.

3. Have students pick out which of the versions is correct and write the correct spelling of the word.

Alphabetize

1. Have students write the Words to Learn in alphabetical order.

2. Note any words that students spelled incorrectly, and correct the spelling errors with students.

Spelling Stairs

Have students write each of the Words to Learn in a stair-step pattern. Be sure that students write neatly so the pattern can be seen.

```
b
b   e   l
b   e   l   l
b   e   l   l   s
```

Word Pyramids

Have students write each of the Words to Learn in a word pyramid. Be sure that students write neatly so that the pyramid shape can be seen.

```
        p
      p   a
    p   a   s
  p   a   s   s
```

Guess the Word

1. Say any letter from one of the Words to Learn. Ask students to guess which word you are thinking of.

2. Say a second letter in the word, a third, and so on until students correctly guess your word.

3. After students guess the word, have them spell that word aloud.

4. Repeat the activity with several words.

Guess the Word Reversed

1. Have students say any letter from one of the Words to Learn. Try to guess which word students are thinking of.

2. Have students say a second letter in the word, a third, and so on until you're able to correctly guess their word.

3. After you guess the word, have students spell that word aloud.

4. Repeat the activity with several words.

Hidden Picture

1. Have students draw a picture and "hide" as many of the Words to Learn as they can inside the picture.

2. See if you or others can find the words within the picture. (The example picture has the spelling words *can*, *fix*, *fun*, and *red* hidden in it.)

3. Note any words that students spelled incorrectly, and correct the spelling errors with students.

Word Scramble

1. Write the letters of each of the Words to Learn in scrambled order.

2. Have students write the correctly spelled word next to each of your scrambled words.

Spelling Scene

Have students draw a picture representing as many of the Words to Learn as they can. Students should label the picture with the spelling words.

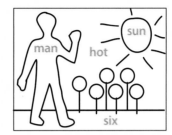

Dots

1. Have students write each of the Words to Learn using dots to form each letter.

2. Have students connect the dots to make the spelling words.

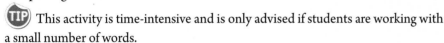

TIP This activity is time-intensive and is only advised if students are working with a small number of words.

Rhymes

1. Have students write each of the Words to Learn.

2. Next to each word, have them write a rhyming word.

3. If there is time, have students try to come up with more than one rhyming word for some of the Words to Learn.

TIP Students may come across rhyming words that are from different word families and are spelled with different spelling conventions (such as *half* and *laugh*). These rhymes are valid, but discuss the differences in the spellings with students.

Crosswords

1. Have students write one of the Words to Learn in the center of a sheet of paper.

2. Have them write another of the Words to Learn by going across and sharing a letter with the first word. See how many words students can connect.

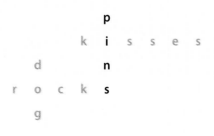

Roll the Number Cube

1. Have students roll the number cube.

2. Have students write one of the Words to Learn the number of times indicated by their roll.

3. Continue the process, having students roll the cube and write a word that many times, until they've written all the Words to Learn.

4. Note any words that students spelled incorrectly, and correct the spelling errors with students.

[Materials]

- household objects – six-sided number cube (labeled 1 through 6)

Snowman

1. Draw a snowman with three circles for the body and head, two eyes, a nose, and hands (see example).

2. Pick one of the Words to Learn, but do not tell students which word you have chosen.

3. Draw one blank space under the snowman for each letter of the word.

4. Ask students to guess what letters might be in the word you have chosen.

5. Each time students make an incorrect guess, erase one part of the snowman. The object of the game is for students to try and guess the whole word before the snowman melts.

Finger Spelling

1. With students turned away from you, tell them you will be spelling one of the Words to Learn on their back with your finger.

2. Using one finger, trace each letter of one of the Words to Learn on the back of a student. Ask the student to guess what word you are spelling.

3. To extend the activity, have students take a turn spelling words on your back.

Spelling Search

1. Have students search for the Words to Learn in newspapers, books, or magazines.

2. Have them write down each word as they find it.

[Materials]

- household objects (optional) – newspaper, book, magazine